Psalm 138:8 (ESV) ~ The Lord will fulfill his purpose
for me; your steadfast love, O Lord, endures forever.
Do not forsake the work of your hands.

Notes

1. Peterson, C., & Seligman, M. E. P. (2004). *Character strengths and virtues: A handbook and classification.* New York: Oxford University Press and Washington, DC: American Psychological Association.
2. Scripture quotations marked (NIV) are taken from the Holy Bible, New International Version®, NIV®. Copyright © 1973, 1978, 1984, 2011 by Biblica, Inc.™ Used by permission of Zondervan. All rights reserved worldwide. www.zondervan.com The "NIV" and "New International Version" are trademarks registered in the United States Patent and Trademark Office by Biblica, Inc.™
3. Scripture quotations marked (ESV) are from The Holy Bible, English Standard Version® (ESV®), copyright © 2001 by Crossway, a publishing ministry of Good News Publishers. Used by permission. All rights reserved.
4. Scripture quotations marked (NLT) are taken from the Holy Bible, New Living Translation, copyright © 1996, 2004, 2007 by Tyndale House Foundation. Used by permission of Tyndale House Publishers, Inc., Carol Stream, Illinois 60188. All rights reserved.

Visit the author's website *www.andreacrisp.ca*

ISBN-13: 978-0992066000

Cover Design: Stephanie Desloges
Cover Image: iStockphoto, royalty free
Cover Photo: Jenna Jacklin

Preface

A few years ago I faced one of the hardest challenges of my life. I had been let go from a ministry position and decided to pick up, move to a new city and start over. During that time I encountered many opportunities that caused me to take some risks, and yet I felt an overwhelming peace walking through that entire season. One opportunity came in the form of Kathy, who became my Life Purpose Coach. As we worked together to pursue my own certification in Life Purpose Coaching, I began to see that there was so much more for my life if I would only be willing to take risks for my dreams and passions.

I came to an understanding that it is the dreams God has given me, through my relationship with Him, that have encouraged me to pursue who I am ~ who I was created to be. This has given me the courage to inspire other women to push the boundaries of their own lives. Several years ago I set out on a journey with six women for six weeks to discover their God-given purposes, and what happened in the lives of these women astounded me. I found that one of my greatest joys is to see women realize that God has so much more for their lives than they could have ever imagined, and I was inspired to continue to coach women in a group setting. Within this kind of group, it becomes more about how we are each uniquely designed to fulfill a purpose and about how walking the journey together can empower us to greatness. When we are able to truly be vulnerable with one another and share the journey, God does the miraculous in our lives.

This book is designed to be done in a group context with "purpose" sisters and a coach or trained facilitator, or as a tool for Life Purpose Coaches to use with clients. However, you could also do it with trusted friends who want to pursue this journey. I pray it will be a blessing to you however you choose to use it.

I invite you to join me on this journey to unearth your passions, live inspired, and walk in the purpose you have been designed for.

Acknowledgements

For the women who journeyed with me by sharing their lives and vulnerability, I am forever grateful. All my love to Michelle Lai, Roxanne Ippolito and Carol-Anne Noble who believed more for my life purpose. Your leadership and friendship are second to none.

I am grateful for friends to do life with and who live out their purpose with love. To Peggy Mayhew, who listened to my ramblings and encouraged me towards healing and purpose. To Katie Tenkate, who gave me the space to be creative and threw courage at me with every turn. And, to the Purpose Sisters who believed that the best is yet to come.

Thanks to my editor Anita Christoff, who graciously took on this project and gave me an understanding of how powerful words can be. To my designer Stephanie Desloges, whom I have seen grow into a beautiful woman of purpose. You have inspired me! Without these beautiful souls I would not have been able to take this project to the next level.

To my brother Clayton, who understands the meaning of family and loves deeply and unconditionally. Thanks for being honest and using your humour to help me navigate my own journey. You are without a doubt one of my favourite people on the planet.

All my love to my parents Randy and Karen Crisp. Thank you for believing that I could do something that I thought was impossible. Your enthusiasm as I walked out this project has helped me stay the course. Thanks for the endless hours of reading drafts, listening to me go on about the process and keeping me encouraged to finish strong. In everything I put my hand to, you have always believed in me and that is what makes you great parents!

Without my Saviours love I have nothing to give. You are the reason I can pursue this dream with a passion. Jesus, you make this journey worthwhile.

Table of Contents

Section One

Designed With Purpose

"If we did all the things we are capable of doing,
we would literally astound ourselves."
~ *Thomas Edison*

God has crafted you uniquely, and has a specific plan for your life. It's exciting to know that we each have our own path, and no two are alike. So many of our life experiences and the difficult situations we encounter form the character of our personhood. Have you ever wondered why you are wired a certain way to enjoy certain tasks or are oriented to be stronger at some areas and not others? What things do you enjoy doing, and what are you passionate about? Maybe you are fully aware of the things you excel at, or maybe you find it difficult to pinpoint strengths. Often we overlook our own character strengths and focus on weak areas, hoping we'll be able to change them. I'm so glad that God has a specific plan for my life, one that can only be carried out by me. When I begin to focus on the strengths of my character instead of on my weaknesses, I am able to see all the ways that God has changed my life and helped me to grow into a more mature woman.

One of my character strengths is honesty, but I sometimes get myself into trouble by being much too blunt in certain situations. And sometimes I give my two cents when it is not appropriate. This happens more than I would like it to. It has become a delicate balance to use my honesty properly so that it is a strength, and to realize that when it is not used properly, it can be my greatest weakness. Even though I believe God created me with the ability to speak truth, He also desires to trust me with it so that situations in my life will bring Him glory and edify other people.

> *For I want you to understand what really matters, so that you may live pure and blameless lives until the day of Christ's return. May you be always be filled with the fruit of your salvation - the righteous character produced in your life by Jesus Christ - for this will bring much glory and praise to God. ~ Philippians 1:10-12 (NLT)*

This scripture is such a great word to pray over yourself daily. When we feel tempted to be down on ourselves, it is such a wonderful reminder that our character is produced through our relationship with Jesus and that He desires our strengths to bring glory and honour to God. In the following sentence, replace my name with yours and begin to speak that over your character: *Andrea, may you always understand what really matters and be filled with the fruit of your salvation ~ the righteous character produced in your life by Jesus Christ ~ for this will bring much glory and praise to God.*

Instead of asking you to try to come up with a list of your character strengths by yourself, I have provided you with a list of character traits that can be found on www.viacharacter.org. These traits are broken down into six categories to help you see which qualities are your strengths.

Go through the list and check off the character traits you possess. When you're finished, place a star beside the top five character strengths that describe you, and make a note of why you believe they're your strongest character traits. Allow yourself the freedom to believe in yourself during this exercise.

Wisdom and Knowledge
Cognitive strengths that entail the acquisition and use of knowledge

Creativity (originality, ingenuity): Thinking of novel and productive ways to conceptualize and do things; includes artistic achievement but is not limited to it.

Curiosity (interest, novelty-seeking, openness to experience): Taking an interest in ongoing experience for its own sake; finding subjects and topics fascinating; exploring and discovering.

Judgment (critical thinking): Thinking things through and examining them from all sides; not jumping to conclusions; being able to change one's mind in light of evidence; weighing all evidence fairly.

Love of Learning: Mastering new skills, topics, and bodies of knowledge, whether on one's own or formally; obviously related to the strength of curiosity but goes beyond it to describe the tendency to add systematically to what one knows.

Perspective (wisdom): Being able to provide wise counsel to others; having ways of looking at the world that make sense to oneself and to other people.

Courage
Emotional strengths that involve the exercise of will to accomplish goals in the face of opposition, external or internal

Bravery (valour): Not shrinking from threat, challenge, difficulty, or pain; speaking up for what's right even if there is opposition; acting on convictions even if unpopular; includes physical bravery, but is not limited to it.

Perseverance (persistence, industriousness): Finishing what one starts; persisting in a course of action in spite of obstacles; "getting it out the door"; taking pleasure in completing tasks.

Honesty (authenticity, integrity): Speaking the truth, but more broadly, presenting oneself in a genuine way and acting in a sincere way; being without pretense; taking responsibility for one's feelings and actions.

Zest (vitality, enthusiasm, vigour, energy): Approaching life with excitement and energy; not doing things halfway or halfheartedly; living life as an adventure; feeling alive and activated.

Humanity
Interpersonal strengths that involve tending and befriending others

Love: Valuing close relations with others, in particular those in which sharing and caring are reciprocated; being close to people.

Kindness (generosity, nurturance, care, compassion, altruistic love, "niceness"): Doing favours and good deeds for others; helping them; taking care of them.

Social Intelligence (emotional intelligence, personal intelligence): Being aware of the motives and feelings of other people and oneself; knowing what to do to fit into different social situations; knowing what makes other people tick.

Justice
Civic strengths that underlie healthy community life

Teamwork (citizenship, social responsibility, loyalty): Working well as a member of a group or team; being loyal to the group; doing one's share.

Fairness: Treating all people the same according to notions of fairness and justice; not letting personal feelings bias decisions about others; giving everyone a fair chance.

Leadership: Encouraging a group of which one is a member to get things done while maintaining good relations within the group; organizing group activities and ensuring they happen.

Temperance
Strengths that protect against excess

Forgiveness: Forgiving those who have done wrong; accepting the shortcomings of others; giving people a second chance; not being vengeful.

Humility: Letting one's accomplishments speak for themselves; not regarding oneself as more special than one is.

Prudence: Being careful about one's choices; not taking undue risks; not saying or doing things that might later be regretted.

Self-Regulation (self-control): Regulating what one feels and does; being disciplined; controlling one's appetites and emotions.

Transcendence

Strengths that forge connections to the larger universe and provide meaning

_____ Appreciation of Beauty and Excellence (awe, wonder, elevation): Noticing and appreciating beauty, excellence, and/or skilled performance in various domains of life, from nature to art to mathematics to science to everyday experience.

_____ Gratitude: Being aware of and thankful for the good things that happen; taking time to express thanks.

_____ Hope (optimism, future-mindedness, future orientation): Expecting the best in the future and working to achieve it; believing that a good future is something that can be brought about.

_____ Humour (playfulness): Liking to laugh and tease; bringing smiles to other people; seeing the light side; making (not necessarily telling) jokes.

_____ Spirituality (faith, purpose): Having coherent beliefs about the higher purpose and meaning of the universe; knowing where one fits within the larger scheme; having beliefs about the meaning of life that shape conduct and provide comfort.

From the list, write the top five character strengths you placed a star beside:

1. _____

2. _____

3. _____

4. _____

5. _____

Were you able to pinpoint your strengths, or did you find it difficult to clearly assess what you excel at? In the space below, write your thoughts about the findings of this test.

_____

_____

_____

_____

If you want to have a more comprehensive understanding of your character strengths, you can take the online test at *https://viame.org/survey/Account/Register.*

Compare your results with your original top five. Be sure to print off a copy and bring it to class so you can share your results with us.

Wherever You Go, I Will Go

**"God is more interested in your future and your
relationships than you are."**
~ Billy Graham

We long for them, cry over them, and spend enormous amounts of time investing in them. Relationships can rescue us from our painful past, mend a lonely heart, and provide a listening ear during times of crisis. There is nothing quite like the feeling of having someone in your life who knows you, understands the quirky things as well as the not-so-loveable things about you, and yet loves you all the same. When we get to that place in a relationship where we find freedom to be ourselves, and know that we are loved, it seems as though we can do anything. My family knows me better than anyone, and yet still loves me. On the days when I wake up grouchy, and don't want to talk for the first hour of the day, they give me space to just be. They are also the people that celebrate with me the special moments of my life ~ like when I graduated with my Master's degree, and when I crossed the finish line of my very first 10k race.

I cherish the relationships I have with my mom and dad, and have always been close to both of them. I have always been able to count on them through good and bad. It was my folks who drove the 21 hours from Ottawa to Springfield, Missouri to help me with one of the most monumental moments in my undergraduate education. As a music education major, I had been preparing for over three years for my senior voice recital, and was finally about to walk centre stage and showcase all of my hard work. It was late November, and the weather had turned unusually wet and cold. The roads were covered with ice, and I was scheduled to have all of my peers and professors come and be a part of my final project. Stress was mounting and I began to wonder if it would be better if I just postponed the recital for another time. Instead of calling things off, my parents rallied the troops and drove all over the city that afternoon to make sure my reception was absolutely perfect. And that night they sat through my recital beaming with pride.

The relationships we have with significant people in our lives define who we become, and affect us for change and transformation. I am blessed with so many wonderful relationships that I have been able to draw strength and courage from over the years. In fact, I am certain that many of those relationships have given me courage to face difficult situations, and have given me a kick in the butt when needed.

I never could have imagined that a friendship that would begin in my childhood would forever change how I look at relationships. I remember as a nine-year-old sitting beside my babysitter Rosanna, at my piano in the dining room of my home, as a relationship formed that would define who I am today. With fond memories, I recall the many times we played that piano together, and how I grew in character with her by my side. She was my very first mentor, and during my younger years, I did not realize the importance of the relationship that was transpiring between us. But, over many years Rosanna became the person in whom I confided all my hopes and dreams. She was the first person I told when I was called into ministry, and when I was filled with the baptism of the Holy Spirit. And that same young woman would eventually teach me to drive stick shift, give me advice about boys, and push me to risk more than I felt capable of. A relationship to last a lifetime.

One of my favourite relationships in the Bible is found in the book of Ruth. It is a beautiful story of two women ~ one young, one older ~ whose lives are bound together by life circumstance and tragedy. Ruth and Naomi develop such a beautiful relationship, even though they are not related by blood. Naomi had lived with her two sons and their wives, Ruth and Orpah, since the death of Naomi's husband. Later, both of Naomi's sons also died, leaving her to grieve with her two daughters-in-law. Naomi told both women to go back to their respective families so that each would be cared for, but Ruth refused to leave Naomi. She decided to stay with her mother-in-law so that she would be supported for the remainder of her life. What an incredible story of friendship and loyalty. It also has a bit of romance in there as well. Take some time this week to sit down with your Bible, a cup of coffee, and read through the entire book of Ruth. You will not be disappointed by a relationship that propelled both women into their destiny.

> *"Don't ask me to leave you and turn back. Wherever you go, I will go; wherever you live, I will live. Your people will be my people, and your God will be my God. Wherever you die, I will die, and there I will be buried. May the Lord punish me severely if I allow anything but death to separate us!" When Naomi saw that Ruth was determined to go with her, she said nothing more.*
> *~ Ruth 1:16-18 (NLT)*

As you look over the course of your life from childhood through adolescence and onto adulthood, many relationships probably stand out to you that have shaped you into who you are today. Maybe it was a teacher in elementary school who helped you learn something that you were unable to understand. Perhaps it was a volleyball coach who practised with you after all the other kids had gone home. Often these special relationships are found close to home, with a sibling or a parent. It is important to recognize these relationships in our lives, so that we can define how we have grown and changed because of them.

Think about three pivotal people in your life who have compelled you to become a better person. Take a moment to write down how these people have impacted you. Don't rush through the process of writing down the ways in which these people have touched your life. Allow yourself some time to reflect on how they have brought about transformation in your life.

16

#1.

_____

_____

_____

_____

_____

_____

#2.

_____

_____

_____

_____

_____

#3.

_____

_____

_____

_____

_____

have taken the time to write about a few of the amazing people
et's go a little further by taking a few moments to write a personal
of these special people. Every so often, I receive a hand-written card
from my spiritual grandmother, Ms. Corrine, who lives in Memphis,
I love how she takes time and care to write me scriptures and prayers
so that I can look at them and be encouraged even though she lives
far away.

Carve out some time this week to sit down, put pen to paper, and write a letter to someone you cherish in your life. Imagine how they will feel when they open the mailbox and find a hand-written letter from you. Before you mail it out, make a copy so you can keep it as a reminder of what they mean to you. Bring the letter to class because you may have an opportunity to share a portion of it with the other ladies. Have fun with this assignment!

Purpose Group Story:
This letter-writing assignment had a significant impact on a woman in one of my past classes. She had shared how a Sunday School teacher had made a huge deposit in her life. After our class, she took the time to write a letter to her former teacher, who was now very late in life. A few weeks later, it just so happened that she went to a service honouring the teacher's late husband, and was able to hand-deliver the letter to the children of this great woman of God. You can only imagine what happened after that. Her children were able to hear of how their mother had changed a life. Talk about having a far-reaching impact!

Daughters

**"I will be a Father to you, and you will be my sons
and daughters, says the Lord Almighty."**
~ 2 Corinthians 6:18 (NIV)

When I was a little girl, we had a small room in the basement that housed old furniture, including a couple of schoolhouse desks. You know, the kind that open from the top and have initials etched into the wood. They were awesome! On many occasions, I would pretend that I was a school teacher and make my younger brother sit while I "taught" him. I vividly remember playing the role of teacher, and I absolutely loved it. During all of those play times, I didn't realize that it would be a precursor to my eight-year teaching career.

We each play different roles in our lives, and sometimes find those roles shift and change with varying seasons. We go from playing the role of daughter to that of mother, sister, friend, co-worker, girlfriend or wife. And these are just some of the roles in which we can find ourselves.

In my own life, I play the role of daughter, sister, friend, confidante, coach, mentor, pastor, teacher, cousin and granddaughter. One of the most important roles that I play (and that I too often overlook) is my role as daughter of the King. I am an heir to the Kingdom of God, a daughter of the Most High God. And of all the roles I fill, this is the most important.

Purpose Group Story:

I had the great opportunity to meet and pray with one of the beautiful women who have been a part of Purpose Group. She shared with me about how God had been speaking to her that she was not a slave to the King, but a daughter of the King. What a magnificent realization! We belong as daughters to a King. *The* King!

What are some of the roles you play in your life? How do you feel about these roles? Are you happy with them? Let's examine these roles, and ask God how He can transform us in these roles. Maybe you find one role to be particularly exhausting. Is God speaking to you about a role you need to give up? If you want to see growth in one or more of these roles, make a note so that we can talk about it together.

Circle all of the roles that you fill in the list below:

daughter	employee	mother
employer	volunteer	counsellor
mentor	granddaughter	grandmother
friend	team leader	actor
pastor	cousin	musician
church member	coach	athlete
sibling	"taxi driver"	executive
wife	girlfriend	board member
fiancée	aunt	teacher

One of the more challenging and yet rewarding roles I have played in my life is the role of pastor. Being a woman in the role of a pastor is difficult in the sense that there are not that many women pastors to learn from and to watch how they grew in that role. I have had to research, ask questions and find other women to help me in this role. And although it has been hard at times, I absolutely love being a woman in ministry. Although now and then I feel like walking away from it, I count it a privilege to serve in this role, even if it is the most difficult one I have.

Questions:

1. Think about one of the more difficult roles you have played. Share how you have navigated your way through that role during a tough assignment.

_____

_____

_____

_____

2. Define your role as daughter of the King. What part do you play in your relationship with God? Do you desire this to change?

_____

_____

_____

_____

3. Is there a role that God is asking you to step into, but that you are hesitating about? What steps can you take toward stepping into that role?

4. Are you happy with the roles in your life?

5. Is God speaking to you about a role you need to give up?

6. Is there a role in which you desire to see growth? Describe the current role you play ~ and allow yourself the freedom to dream about what it could look like in the future.

The Way, the Truth, the Life

> "All I have seen teaches me to trust the
> Creator for all I have not seen."
> ~ *Ralph Waldo Emerson*

When I was a little girl, I came to know Jesus Christ as my personal Saviour in my bedroom one summer night after church. It was not a radical conversion where my life completely changed from being a life full of sin and shame to that of a redeemed person. I was only a young girl, probably around the age of seven, so really, what could I have done that was so sinful to cause my life to change so completely? And yet, it did! For as long as I can remember I have found the answer, and my cause, in the death and resurrection of Jesus Christ. I live a redeemed life, and it is only because of Jesus, who was fully God and yet fully man. He led a sinless life, gave His life for mine by death on a cross and through His resurrection I have freedom. I have victory!

Since my childhood, I have matured in my faith and now understand the changing relationship that I have with the Trinity (God, Jesus and Holy Spirit). By knowing God as Father, I am able to understand the true nature of the authority I possess through Him. Because of His great love for me and my relationship with Jesus, I have the freedom to be authentic. The indwelling of the Holy Spirit in my life gives me the guidance and direction to make decisions so I can live my life righteously and victoriously. Not through my own strength, but through the Great Helper's strength.

What we believe about our relationship with Christ and the power of the Holy Spirit will shape our view of the future, and what we can believe God for. This is a great place to take some time to evaluate where your relationship stands. Perhaps you have never thought about your relationship being three-fold ~ with Father, Son and Holy Spirit. But without the working of each in our lives we cannot be fully operating in the fullness intended for our lives.

My earthly father is my earthly hero, and I am blessed to have a great relationship with him. Since I was a little girl, I have been able to share anything with my dad. And when I say anything, I really do mean that. He has allowed me to become the woman of purpose that God intended for my life by giving me boundaries, advice and instruction ~ and by having a good sense of humour! Our relationship is stronger today than it has ever been, and I am so grateful to have a father like him. But many women have not had the same experience with their earthly fathers. Unfortunately, they have been hurt by their fathers in ways that are so harmful and hurtful that it has taken years of healing to come to terms with their childhood. And that can have a lasting impact on how they see their relationship with God the Father.

What is your belief about God as your father? In your own words, describe your relationship with Him.

_____

_____

_____

_____

_____

_____

Jesus was the son of God, and came to earth to be the ultimate sacrifice and atonement for our sinful nature. It always astounds me that one man carried the entire weight of the world on Himself by death on a cross so that we can spend eternity with Him. The Bible says that the way to God only comes through relationship with Jesus.

> **_Jesus answered, "I am the way and the truth and the life. No one comes to the Father except through me." ~ John 14:6 (NIV)_**

Our view of our relationship with Jesus is key to living a life as an overcomer ~ a victor, not a victim. Be honest in your view of your relationship with Jesus as your Saviour. If you have never allowed him to be the centre of your life, then this may be a time where you would like to ask Him to take the reins.

Who is Jesus Christ to you?

_____

_____

_____

_____

_____

_____

My relationship with the Holy Spirit has grown and matured over the years as I have allowed myself to be in true connection with him. As I allow Him to guide and help me, I can see how this relationship is the one that equips me to make wise decisions for my life, and gives me insight into things I would otherwise not understand.

When Jesus left His disciples, He told them He had to leave this earth in order for the Holy Spirit to take residence on the earth. That amazes me. If I were a disciple, I would have wanted Jesus to stay with me forever so that I could have access to His knowledge, His healing power and His ability to save. But He told them that He was going so that the Holy Spirit would empower them to do things that would never be possible while He was on Earth.

> *But very truly I tell you, it is for your good that I am going away. Unless I go away, the Advocate will not come to you; but if I go, I will send him to you. When He comes, He will prove the world to be in the wrong about sin and righteousness and judgment: about sin, because people do not believe in me; about righteousness, because I am going to the Father, where you can see me no longer; and about judgment, because the prince of this world now stands condemned. I have much more to say to you, more than you can now bear. But when He, the Spirit of Truth, comes, He will guide you into all truth. He will not speak on His own; He will speak only what He hears, and He will tell you what is yet to come. He will glorify me because it is from me that He will receive what He will make known to you. All that belongs to the Father is mine. That is why I said the Spirit will receive from me what He will make known to you.*
> *~ John 16:7-15 (NIV)*

What is your understanding of the Holy Spirit in your life? Do you desire for this relationship to grow in understanding? Describe your relationship with the Holy Spirit.

_____

_____

_____

_____

_____

Section Two

A Great Pair of Jeans

**The purposes of a person's heart are deep waters,
but one who has insight draws them out.**
~ Proverbs 20:5 (NIV)

Whether good or bad, I think that we are all motivated to do things in our lives. Sometimes these motives have a healthy quality to them, but sometimes we can find ourselves motivated by hidden negative things. Personally, I am motivated by creativity ~ well, that and fitting into a great pair of jeans! Fortunately, at work I am encouraged to be creative, and am able to get a lot more accomplished when I can work out of my creativity.

However, as I mentioned, I am also motivated by a great pair of jeans. And because of this, and my quest to get fit and become a much healthier version of myself, I have taken to going to the gym at least five days a week. Many might think this is a form of torture, but I have grown fond of the time I spend in the gym! On my way there one afternoon, I came across an older gentleman who noticed I was on my way to work out. As we were in an elevator and had 25 floors to go, we chatted for a few minutes, and he told me he had just run a marathon. I was extremely impressed by his accomplishment, especially because at that time I would consider it a good day if I ran for 15 minutes straight without falling over dead on the treadmill. Right before the doors opened and I was about to get off, he said something that has stayed with me:

> *"Picture yourself where you want to be instead of where you are today." ~ Random Stranger*

What motivates you? Is it the possibility of a job promotion, or the reward of a piece of chocolate cake? Are you sent into action by stress, or the ability to change the world?

In a previous chapter we looked at the book of Ruth and the relationship between Naomi and Ruth. I have never been married or lost a husband or sons, but of course it would be devastating, especially in a time where women depended on men for their financial stability. In the story, Ruth later meets Boaz, a relative of Naomi, and finds favour with him as she works in his field. Boaz recognizes all that Ruth has done to help her mother-in-law and decides that he will share with her what the workers have gathered. He even tells his workers not to give her a hard time when she is in the field. In other words, he was telling them that she was "special" and "protected." In time, following Naomi's advice, Ruth goes to Boaz and when he falls asleep, she lies at his feet. What a surprise for him to wake up and find her at the end of his bed. Since Boaz was a man of integrity, and did not want anyone to think Ruth was a woman of low morals, he decided to go into the town and buy the land of her ancestors, and asked Ruth to be his wife.

> *So Boaz took Ruth into his home, and she became his wife. When he slept with her, the Lord enabled her to become pregnant, and she gave birth to a son. Then the women of the town said to Naomi, "Praise the Lord who has provided a redeemer for your family! May this child be famous in Israel. May he restore your youth and care for you in your old age. For he is the son of your daughter-in-law who loves you and has been better to you than seven sons!"*
> *~ Ruth 4:13-15 (NLT)*

Wow!! What a story! Although most of us could not imagine ourselves surreptitiously sleeping at the feet of a man in order to prompt him to propose, Ruth was motivated by something so great that she would do anything to achieve it. She loved her mother-in-law so greatly that she wanted to provide for them both. By marrying Boaz, she was able to do more that she could have ever imagined. Not to mention that she went on to have David in her family lineage.

We are motivated by various things, and not always in a good way. What are some of the motives of your heart? In the space below, list three negative or positive motives that have led you to success.

1.

2.

_____

_____

_____

_____

_____

_____

3.

_____

_____

_____

_____

_____

_____

Questions:
1. Do you have impure motives? List a few examples.

_____

_____

_____

_____

_____

2. Think about someone you tend to treat poorly. What ugly motive in your heart causes you to disregard the value of that relationship?

_____

_____

_____

_____

_____

3. What are some steps you can take to help yourself begin treating this relationship with more respect?

_____

_____

_____

_____

_____

Setting Your Priorities

"It's not hard to make decisions when you know
what your values are." ~ *Roy Disney*

As I'm writing this, I'm sitting at home after a long day with a candle burning and only the sound of the keyboard and my thoughts. Nothing revives me more than being home alone to refresh my senses. I value my time alone and find that I need a full day each week to be by myself and have my "introvert" time. As a pastor, I spend the majority of my time with other people ~ talking, counselling and leading. This can leave me depleted, but one day on my own and I am rejuvenated and ready to face anything that comes my way!

I also cherish the time I spend with my family. I absolutely love the sound of laughter that comes from our house when my family is together. The loud belly laughs that come from being with one another are invigorating. Even when we're not all getting along, I can't wait for the next time that we will all be together. I value my time with family very much.

When you don't know what you value, however, it can be difficult to set your priorities. And, as women, there are so many things and people vying for our time and attention. Defining our values is an integral part of gaining understanding of our purpose and destiny. When we are able to pinpoint our values, then we experience a more balanced expectation of the relationships and people in our lives. It can also keep us from making bad choices. If we know our values, then we become aware of our decisions that are in direct conflict with them.

When we are able to determine the core values that govern our lives, there is a freedom to pursue the God-given purpose we each have inside of us. It gives us the ability to access courage and motivation to step out of our comfort zones and do things we would never have expected of ourselves.

I have written an extensive list of values. By no means are all possible values included, as there are hundreds. But I hope you will find these helpful to you.

Check off the values that are important to you. Some of these may be in conflict with each other, so really think about which one is more important. As an example, you may really love to travel but your financial security is also a priority. How do they work against each other? Can you find a way to make them work together?

acceptance	happiness	recognition
accomplishment	health	reputation
affection	holiness	respect
appreciation	honesty	responsibility
approval	hospitality	satisfaction
balance	humility	self-control
beauty	independence	sensitivity
challenge	influence	service
cleanliness	inspiration	significance
community	integrity	solitude
compassion	intelligence	spirituality
confidence	intimacy	success
courage	kindness	support
creativity	knowledge	teamwork
discipline	learning	thankfulness
education	love	thoughtfulness
empathy	loyalty	traditionalism
encouragement	optimism	travel
excellence	order	trust
faith	organization	truth
family	outdoors	understanding
fashion	passion	unity
financial freedom	patience	vision
fitness	peace	vitality
forgiveness	perfection	wealth
friends	perseverance	wisdom
fulfillment	popularity	youthfulness
generosity	pride	zeal
God	professionalism	
gratitude	punctuality	

Questions:
1. What are your top 10 values that you immediately recognize from this list?

_____

_____

_____

_____

_____

2. Are there any other values not mentioned that you would like to add to the list?

_____

_____

_____

_____

3. Were you surprised by the list, or were you expecting those specific values to rise to the top of the list?

_____

_____

_____

_____

Showcase Your Ability

"I would be a fool to deny my own abilities."
~ Julie Andrews

My mom always tells the story of when we were at our family reunion when I was just a toddler. That year she entered me into the kiddie talent show to showcase my singing abilities. (In other words, my cuteness.) I have been told that ever since I could talk, I could sing. So there I was up on a stage singing, "Twinkle, Twinkle." But I did not remember how to end the song and kept starting over at the beginning. What started as a very short little song turned into several refrains. Eventually my mom came up and sang the end with me. I was born to sing. No one had to tell me, it was just a natural thing for me to do. But I did have to make the choice when I got older to keep singing and to take lessons. It was my decision to pursue music in college.

You may already have a handle on what you are naturally gifted to do, but perhaps you put that ability on the shelf to pursue other things. Or maybe you were never encouraged to pursue your natural abilities and had to do something less desirable. This is a great time to really take stock of what you are naturally inclined to do, or what you have become good at through practice or experience and now enjoy.

So often we focus on the things we cannot do, and while spending time trying to improve those skills, we forget to do the things we are gifted to do. We have all been given a set of talents and abilities that we use every day, or have learned to use through our education. Check off all of the abilities you possess. This is a great way to see where you excel.

____ public speaking	____ graphics	____ audio productions
____ writing	____ daycare	____ interior design
____ editing	____ public relations	____ decorating
____ critical thinking	____ photography	____ video creation
____ math	____ relaxation	____ web design
____ recruiting	____ taxes	____ programming
____ dance	____ advertising	____ humour
____ persuasive	____ health/fitness	____ creativity
____ story telling	____ financial management	____ sign language
____ problem solving	____ conflict resolution	____ planning leadership
____ sales		____ landscaping

- evangelism
- acting
- sound mixing
- typing
- composition
- linguistics
- film/television
- science
- beauty
- architecture
- maintenance
- human resources
- counselling
- social work
- accounting
- medical
- law enforcement
- painting
- musician
- nursing
- script writer
- helps
- tutoring
- pottery
- investor
- management
- modelling
- care of animals
- teaching
- cooking
- set design/ construction
- singing
- advertising
- pastoral
- journalism
- legal
- entertainer
- dental
- missions
- coaching
- mental services
- food service
- sports
- humanitarian
- fashion
- gardening
- research

Note any other abilities you possess that are not on the list:

_____

_____

_____

_____

_____

You Can Overcome

**In Him we were also chosen, having been predestined
according to the plan of him who works out everything
in conformity with the purpose of His will.**
~ Ephesians 1:11 (NIV)

So many people have different reasons for not accomplishing purpose in their lives; when traced back to *why*, it often comes down to being fearful of something. Fear of not being able to stand out in a crowd; being insignificant, or even growing old. One friend even told me that she is afraid of not being able to accomplish goals set before her.

Fears can cause us anxiety, can keep us from sleep, and even stop us from really accomplishing all that God has set out for our lives. There have been moments in my own life where I have allowed fear to swallow me whole and rule my life. One of the hardest realizations for me was that I was giving in to those fears and letting them rule me, instead of allowing God to be my cornerstone.

One of my dear friends, a married woman and mother of three, wrote to me with her story:

> *"I never really struggled with fear until I was married. Then I began having panic attacks. In my youth, I travelled to different countries, jumped off cliffs, swam in the middle of the ocean, took risks, had adventurous experiences ~ so I never thought I would experience this. It was a month after I got married that I had my first panic attack. My legs were especially affected; they just stopped working. I immediately began to cry and plead with God. Finally I began to command it to stop. As the years continued, and with the birth of my first child, I became a regular at the walk-in clinic with symptoms of heart burn, acid reflux, and heart palpitations. I wondered if I was having a heart attack, perhaps even going to die. During this time I had my first miscarriage and my body once again went out of control as I began to hallucinate, being too fearful to even sleep. When I found out I was pregnant, and carried to term my second child, I knew that she had come and saved my life. At a women's conference, I received a prophetic word about my life and the lives of my girls. God was healing me and I was being transformed with hope for myself and for my daughters. I never want my daughters to have to walk down that road, and because of that, I am determined to share my story. God brought me out of darkness, and healed me and deserves all the glory and praise. I now have three beautiful daughters and I pray they will all walk in the destiny God has for them without fear."*

Another of my good friends has a fear of speaking in front of a crowd. We have talked at length about this fear, and she has expressed to me that she has a desire to get over the fear of public speaking. Personally, I have never experienced this fear and when I am in front of a group of people I have a God-given ability to talk to them. But for my friend, the idea of public speaking causes her great anxiety. She has come a long way in stepping out of her comfort zone, confronting the fear and allowing herself to face it head on. One of the ways she has been able to do this is by taking public speaking classes where she is given the opportunity to grow. In fact, there are times where I am now able to ask her to come and talk in front of a group of people, and she speaks clearly and with an incredible sense of peace. She is conquering her fear, and I applaud her.

Are you bound by fear? Is there a fear that is keeping you from really pursuing all that God has for you? Spend some time reflecting on what that might be and ask God to help you to face that fear. It may not be easy, but with Him you are not alone.

Now that we have begun to take a look at what has held us back from walking with purpose, and have identified a fear that has taken root in our lives, we can ask God for help in overcoming. It might happen quickly, or even take years to completely overcome, but we know that we can have victory over the enemy. God is for us, and He desires that we walk without fear.

The word of God is rich with encouragement about how God is "for us." In times of fear in my own life, I have taken to the scriptures to meditate on how much God loves me, and how He is fully invested in my life. Here are a few scriptures to meditate on over the next week. Ask God to plant these words deep in your spirit so that you will be able to walk them out in your everyday life.

Take a moment and copy these scriptures in your own writing:

He reached down from Heaven and rescued me; He drew me out of deep waters.
~ Psalm 18:16 (NLT)

How precious are your thoughts about me, O God. They cannot be numbered! I can't even count them; they outnumber the grains of sand! And when I wake up, you are still with me!
~ Psalm 139:17-18 (NLT)

For the Lord your God is the one who goes with you to fight for you against your enemies to give you victory. ~ Deuteronomy 20:4 (NIV)

You may have other scriptures that come to mind; write them in the space below as a way of encouraging yourself, and then share them with the class.

Section Three

Making Good Habits, Breaking Bad Habits

**"Good habits formed at youth
make all the difference."**
~ Aristotle

Habits are formed by doing something repeatedly over time, and they generally become a part of our everyday routine. Several years ago I began running, and over the past eight months I have really begun to increase the intensity of my running. I never imagined that I would get to the point where I almost have to go for a run every couple of days, but I have! Now I desire the time where I lace up my running shoes and step outside and feel the fresh air on my face. Not only have I gotten into the habit of running, but it has become a necessary part of my life. When I fall into the rhythm of each step, I begin processing my thoughts and work out problem areas within my life. Good habits can be excellent ways to help us relieve stress and find peace.

Bad habits can include smoking, stress eating / overeating, overspending, trying to be in control, watching TV too much, and the list goes on. The problem with having bad habits in our lives is that we tend to lean into them when we encounter stressful situations, and instead of focusing our energy on something healthy, we gravitate toward something that dulls our senses.

Have you ever wanted to break a bad habit? I know I sure have, whether it is something that is particularly harmful to my body, or something that I know has a negative influence in my life. Not long ago I decided that I would take 30 days and fast one of my favourite beverages: coffee. Now, if you are a serious coffee drinker, you will be able to relate to this. Part of my problem was not only trying to get off caffeine, but dealing with the moodiness that accompanied my lack of caffeine. One of my favourite things to do with friends is sit and chat over a cup of coffee, and for 30 days I had to find some sort of substitute. I am proud to say that I not only made it 30 days, but added an additional five days.

We tend to form habits in our everyday life that can become a hindrance to being able to find our purpose. Some habits, more than others, can be very detrimental to our lives and cause us or our family member great pain. Are there habits in your own life that you have formed that you wish were different?

Spend some time thinking about three good habits that you have formed over the years and write down what motivates you toward them.

Good Habits
1.

_____

_____

_____

2.

_____

_____

_____

3.

_____

_____

_____

Now for the hard part. What are some of the negative habits you have formed? For each one, examine within yourself to see if you have the desire to change any of these habits and improve your life. It may not be easy to change a habit, but with the help of the Holy Spirit, we can leave that habit behind.

Bad Habits
1.

_____

_____

_____

2.

_____

_____

_____

3.

_____

_____

_____

After reflecting on these habits in your life, is there one in particular that you would be able to work toward changing?

_____

_____

_____

What are some steps you can take toward making this a permanent change in your life?

_____

_____

_____

> *You were taught, with regard to your former way of life, to put off your old self, which is being corrupted by its deceitful desires; to be made new in the attitude of your minds; and to put on the new self, created to be like God in true righteousness and holiness.*
> *~ Ephesians 4:22-24 (NIV)*

Breaking Negative Patterns

**"Family love is messy, clinging, and of an annoying
and repetitive pattern, like bad wallpaper."**
~ *P.J. O'Rourke*

All my life I have struggled with my weight; in fact, I can't think of a time when I was not concerned about how I looked or felt in a pair of jeans. I have a vivid memory of myself as a young girl realizing that I was overweight, and eventually it became something that defined me. The problem was compounded by the fact that although I struggled with my weight, I loved food too much. On happy days I wanted to celebrate with it, and on sad days I wanted to be consoled by it. This unhealthy pattern of overeating, and being unhappy with my weight, plagued me for many years.

The struggle with both weight and stress eating runs in my family, and I watched my mother struggle with both of these issues for many years. Even though I saw her struggle, it did not deter me from having the same issue.

Breaking the negative life patterns that we find ourselves entrenched in can be very difficult. Seeing ourselves in the light of who God has made us, and being able to turn toward that truth, is really the only way we will be fully able to break free from the unhealthy cycles and patterns in our lives.

When we begin to identify some of the negative life patterns we can fall into, we are taking the first step in being able to walk in freedom from them. God has designed us with purpose, and desires for us to be able to have positive coping mechanisms and ways of handling stress in our lives that are not destructive and harmful.

One of the ways I deal with the stress in my life is by eliminating any pent-up negative energy. In the morning, generally after I have had a cup of coffee, I go to the gym and work out. I am not going to tell you that I love doing it, but as I have begun to get into the rhythm of this routine, I have grown accustomed to releasing my frustration on the treadmill or the rowing machine. Each morning I am able to process my day, spend time on my own and sow good seed into my life. Now, let me clarify that this is my own personal journey and only what works for me. Finding what works for you is going to be better than anything I could tell you.

Let's begin this part of the journey by identifying some of the negative life patterns that we may have fallen into. Remember, these may be things that come from our family history, or they may be things we have allowed to bind us.

1.

2.

3.

Now that you have dug deep and been honest with yourself about some of the negative patterns in your life, let's explore some ways that you can replace those patterns with healthy patterns. Even though it would be easy to say, "Let's just stop engaging in the old patterns and start with the new ones," we all know it does not work that way. So a good starting point is to look at what scripture tells us about how we should rely on God, and how He can be our source.

> *And the Holy Spirit helps us in our weakness. For example, we don't know what God wants us to pray for. But the Holy Spirit prays for us with groanings that cannot be expressed in words.*
> *~ Romans 8:26 (NLT)*

This scripture is a great example to us of how we should begin to look at overcoming our negative life patterns. Ask the Holy Spirit to help you in your weakness; the scripture tells us that He intercedes on our behalf.

1. Which negative life patterns would you like to interrupt and why?

_____

_____

_____

_____

_____

2. If you had a chance to do something in your life over again, what would it be and why?

_____

_____

_____

_____

_____

Hadassah's Surrender

> "We can only learn to know ourselves and do
> what we can ~ namely, surrender our will
> and fulfill God's will in us."
> ~ *Saint Teresa of Avila*

I want to commend you for digging deep into who you are, and being honest with yourself and others. Part of understanding the purpose God has designed for us is realizing that we have allowed negative life patterns, fears and impure motives in our lives. But what a comfort in knowing that God can redeem us and has a plan for our lives that goes beyond what we can ever hope and imagine.

My friend shared with me her story of surrender. During a time of transition in her life, while trying to find a job, she started looking for a sign that things would turn around. God spoke very clearly to her during this time that He would not allow any other idols to be in place of Him, and that once she was able to surrender this area of her life to Him, He would work it out. Here is an excerpt from her journal:

> *"Everything I have is yours. It fills me with joy to give it to you. However, I cannot release such blessings while they are an idol to you, over Me. The minute the subject of your idolatry or fear loses its grip on you, and you realize that I am the answer to all your wants and desires, then I can give you the world, and you will appreciate such things in their true light, value, and meaning."*

What a wonderful revelation that when we place our trust in God and surrender ourselves to Him, He can open doors to our wildest dreams. About a year ago, I was reintroduced to an amazing woman in the Bible who has her very own book, the book of Esther. Before being called Esther (which means "star"), her name was Hadassah (which means "myrtle tree"). Hadassah lived a life of surrender in a way that we can all learn from. She was a woman of Jewish descent and a cousin to Mordecai who was from the tribe of Benjamin. This is a beautiful story of a woman who was mentored by her cousin Mordecai and was, through a series of events, able to give of herself to save her people.

The story begins with an account of how Queen Vashti, who was married to King Xerxes, publicly defied the King during an important party. Under the law the King had no other choice but to banish her and find a new queen. Many beautiful young women in the kingdom were selected to come to the palace so the King could choose a new queen, and Hadassah was one of them. Her cousin Mordecai instructed her not to reveal her true nationality for fear of what might happen to her. But, Hadassah found favour in the eyes of the palace officials and soon found favour with the King as well. In fact, he fell head over heels in love with her and made her his new queen.

The story unfolds with suspense and intrigue as Hadassah learns to surrender who she was, to become who God called her to be. I encourage you to read the entire story found in the book of Esther. An extraordinary book about a woman who changed an entire nation.

In my own life, I have found that God calls me to continually surrender the parts of myself to Him that have not been yielded to Him. During this past season of my life I have undergone some difficulties, and the Holy Spirit is showing me what it's like to surrender my own desires for the future and to allow Him to design something much more beautiful in my life.

What is God calling you to surrender? It may not be your family or your heritage, but is God calling you to give up control of something so that He can make something beautiful of it? Share below.

A Place of Healing

"Only in the darkness can you see the stars."
~ *Martin Luther King Jr.*

However, as it is written: "What no eye has seen, and no ear
has heard, and what no mind has conceived" the things God
has prepared for those who love Him.
~ *1 Corinthians 2:9 (NIV)*

As I mentioned in the preface to this book, a few years ago I went through one of the most trying experiences of my life. It wasn't just hard; it was completely life-altering for me. Here I thought that I had already faced down some difficult seasons, only to find out they were to get me ready for the big one! Isn't it encouraging to know that we might have to go through the tough stuff to prepare us for the really tough stuff!!

I had been serving as a worship and student ministries pastor, and to say I was under-qualified for the job is an understatement. But I was daily experiencing the grace of God like never before. Funny how that works! At the church, we were undergoing some major leadership transitions, and I was feeling the brunt of some serious mud-slinging toward the pastoral team. Being a naive newbie in the situation, I thought that stuff like this should never happen. Boy, did I have a lot to learn! Over the course of a year we lost several of our lead staff, and were soon operating with a transition pastor. As if my job ~ trying to navigate the seas of student ministry ~ had not been difficult enough, I then found myself also trying to wade through a change in church leadership. Then, just before we were to welcome our brand-new permanent pastor into the church, I got called in for a meeting and told my position had been eliminated. Not only that, but I was told I would not be able to say goodbye to all of my students and leaders. It felt like a wet cold slap in the face. People I had trusted my confidence in and shared my life with had handed me the proverbial pink slip and shown me the door.

During those next few weeks, I was forced to come to grips with what had happened, second-guessing all of my decisions, friendships and even ministry itself. I decided to take a five-week trip to gather myself and get alone with God. He and I needed to have a heart to heart. As I drove those many miles I cried out to Him, got really angry, and said a few choice words over the matter. It's a good thing I was alone in the car!

The crazy thing was, there came a point during the trip that my eyes were opened to see that what had been a potentially damaging experience actually ended up teaching me about healing. There are still moments now when I think back to that time that I have to allow healing to flood over me all over again. Forgiveness, grace and mercy have all become a part of my everyday journey toward something that I desire deeply: to be healed.

You probably have your very own journey to healing. Sometimes it can be quite difficult to revisit the past, but in order to move forward into the destiny God has for us, we really need to allow God to heal those deep wounds in our lives. What are you believing God to heal you from?

_____

_____

_____

_____

_____

_____

Those weeks after I was let go from my job, I did a lot of thinking, praying and talking to people I trusted. God gave me that time to really get things into perspective. It was kind of like my very own "Eat, Pray, Love," minus the romance in the end. What is your next step to healing? Is it getting alone with God, journalling, talking with a trusted friend, or meditating on the word of God? Write down what you sense God is saying to you.

_____

_____

_____

_____

_____

_____

Write a letter to the wounded part of you and encourage yourself toward healing. Speak words of life over yourself. Pray the word of God over your situation, and allow forgiveness, grace and mercy to flow into your wounded soul.

Section Four

Finding Inspiration

"A #2 pencil and a dream can take you anywhere."
~ *Joyce Meyer*

From the stained glass of an ancient cathedral to the simple drawings of a small child, we can find inspiration and beauty. We each see beauty in a different way, and can find the inspiration we need in different sources.

My mother refers to me as a "nester," which means I like to have my surroundings comfortable and feel as though I am home wherever I am. This is probably why I take so much time to create a cozy feel in my office at the church, or light candles when I am somewhere unfamiliar to create an inviting scent. My inspiration often comes from the environment that I work in, and if that environment is not conducive to my creativity, then I usually find somewhere else to work. More than once I have been found at my favourite espresso bar writing on their dark wood table, listening to the sound of chatter of customers and occasionally glancing up at the local artwork on the walls of the cafe.

Inspiration is all around us! We have spent the past few weeks looking into what has kept us from our purpose, but now let's take a look in a different direction. What are the things that inspire us?

What inspires you? Or *who* inspires you? Take time to write about five ways you are inspired. Really push yourself to find things that bring about the creativity in your life.

1.

2.

3.

4.

5.

This week your assignment is to go on an adventure in your local neighborhood and find inspiration in the simple things that bring you joy. Write about what you encountered during this time, and allow the inspiration to push you into your creativity, your purpose. Bring something that represents what you found during your adventure.

Share Your Success

> "Let no feeling of discouragement prey upon you,
> and in the end you are sure to succeed."
> ~ *Abraham Lincoln*

When I was in high school and college, I was what you would call an "average student." I thoughtfully applied myself to subjects I was interested in and tossed aside the information that I believed did not apply to me. Because of my lack of interest in learning, I began to think that I was not smart and frequently labelled myself as such. It was not difficult to assume that I was not the brightest when it came to classroom smarts, as my grade point average in college left a lot to be desired.

It was not until after college, when I was praying with a group of friends before my friend Melody's wedding, that God spoke to me specifically about how I refer to myself. At that point in my journey I had no intention of going back to school for more education, and the thought of spending more time learning did not appeal to me in the least. But God had other plans for me. That night in a hotel room in Branson, Missouri, He used a woman of God to speak a word into my life that altered the course I was on. The word she spoke over me was that I *was* smart, something only God knew I needed to hear. It was my Heavenly Father who designed me and used this experience to remind me of who He had made me to be. Thank God for obedient people who hear from the Lord and speak life into us.

Over the next three years I applied, got accepted, and began my Master's degree in counselling. There were many different miracles along the way, and I attributed all that was happening to the hand of God in my life. I had started out believing a lie about myself ~ that I was not good enough, not intelligent enough to be a good student and to achieve more in my life. After three gruelling years in my program, I had changed in ways I never knew were possible, graduating with a 3.88 GPA and acing my comprehensive exams. But the most important achievement at that time in my life was the realization that I possessed what it took to be successful. God had uniquely created me in a certain fashion, and as I began to tap into the source of that creativity I found help to complete all that He had set before me.

Now is the time to celebrate those monumental successes in your life that have propelled you forward. Perhaps you were a competitive athlete, a talented artist, or the salutatorian of your class. Whatever the successes you have had along the way, let's celebrate them together. When we begin to focus on the ways that we have been able to succeed in our lives, we can look toward the future and believe that there are many more to come.

In the space below, write your story of success. Share how you felt during this time in your life.

Unleash Your Passions

> "Don't ask yourself what the world needs; ask yourself what
> makes you come alive. And then go do that. Because what
> the world needs is people who have come alive."
> ~ *Howard Thurman*

People finding purpose. Music. Church Life. These are three things that I am absolutely over-the-moon passionate about. I spend most of my time thinking about them, I daydream about them, and ultimately they are working their way into my everyday life. I feel blessed that part of my job involves all three of my passions. But not everyone has the opportunity to work in the area of their passions. Do you? What are you passionate about? There must be something that you go wild about when asked.

Months before I began my Master's program, I was at the wedding of my friends Melody and Nate. It had been a very monumental weekend because of some of the healing that had taken place during that time. But something else had happened that was equally important. It was a conversation between my friend's mother and a few of the bridesmaids. We were all chatting at a restaurant when Renee, the mother of the bride, asked us a pointed question: *"If you had unlimited resources and could do anything with your life, what would it be?"*

I had never been asked a question like that, and my mind began to race through all of the things that I would want to do. I was getting excited with the possibilities. That day I saw my life through a different lens, through the lens of my passions and the possibilities of pursuing them.

God has placed within each of us a desire to fulfill our passions. He created us to be creative; after all, we are made in His image. Why should we spend another day without walking in the fullness of who He has made us to be?

Let's go on another adventure, one that allows you to dream and go anywhere in the world you want to go. The sky's the limit. Take off your practical hat, and allow your imagination to take the lead. In this next exercise, begin to write about what you would do with your life if you had unlimited time and resources.

WHERE would you be? WHAT would you be doing? And WHY?

Picture Yourself

"Faith is believing that God is going to take you
places before you even get there."
~ *Matthew Barnett*

Throughout this journey, we have focused on finding out who we were created to be and looked at stories and people in the Bible who exemplified the journey to purpose. Faith is an integral part of that process and is often overlooked. Once we have started on the path to our destiny, we realize there are always going to be obstacles and trials along the way. Just because we have discovered more about the design of our lives does not necessarily mean it will be "smooth sailing."

Let's look at the story of Sarah as an example. Sarah desired more than anything to be a mother and to bless her husband Abraham with a son, an heir. But after many years of barrenness, she lost hope in the promise God had made to her that she would have a son, and took matters into her own hands. She gave her maid Hagar to her husband so that Hagar could produce the heir. As you can imagine, this situation ended up causing pain and trouble for all of them. In spite of this, God did not withhold the promise He had made to Sarah. At the age of 90, Sarah finally gave birth to her purpose and destiny, a son she named Isaac.

> *God also said to Abraham, "As for Sarai your wife, you are no longer to call her Sarai; her name will be Sarah. I will bless her and will surely give you a son by her. I will bless her so that she will be the mother of nations; kings of peoples will come from her."*
> ~ *Genesis 17:15-16 (NIV)*

If only Sarah had exercised her faith from the beginning and waited patiently, perhaps she would not have gone through so much pain. But in the end, she learned from her mistake and walked by faith and not by sight. God had promised her a son, and He came through on His promise.

God will come through on His promise for you as well. Don't worry about the timing, or allow comparison with others hold you back from the purpose He has spoken over your life. Keep your eyes focused on Him, and allow Him to work out the timing. Over the years, I have been walking out my faith journey believing in the promise that God has spoken into my life. There have been times when I was not seeing anything that looked remotely like destiny, and I wanted to throw in the towel. In fact there were times when things seemed so grim that I was ready to walk away from ministry and the call God has on my life. I am always reminding myself to keep believing and to thank God in advance for the things He is doing and going to do in my life.

Earlier on I mentioned the time I had a random conversation with an older gentleman in an elevator about working out. At that time, I had quite a ways to go toward getting fit and healthy. Well, a year has gone by and even to this date I am shocked at the results of the work I have put into going to the gym. Had you asked me over a year ago if I thought I would ever be at this place, I would have told you there would be no way. That conversation in the elevator, including his words, *"Picture yourself where you want to be instead of where you are today,"* has been a constant reminder to me to stay the course. The journey to being fit is far from over, but every day I tell myself that I am one step closer to being who I want to become.

Where are you with your level of faith? Do you need a resurgence of your faith to believe that God is going to work things out in order for your purpose to be realized? Don't give up hope!

> *Not only so, but we also glory in our sufferings, because we know that suffering produces perseverance; perseverance, character; and character, hope. And hope does not put us to shame, because God's love has been poured out into our hearts through the Holy Spirit, who has been given to us. ~ Romans 5:3-5 (NIV)*

Take some time to thank God for what you have gone through, and all that you have learned. He is interested in your journey and wants to hear about it. If you are low on faith, ask Him to renew your faith. Ask Him to help your unbelief so that when discouragement comes you will be able to look toward the great things that He has in store for you.

> *Now faith is confidence in what we hope for and assurance about what we do not see. ~ Hebrews 11:1 (NIV)*

Fullness of God's Love

Because of the Lord's great love we are not consumed, for His compassions never fail. They are new every morning; great is your faithfulness. I say to myself, "The Lord is my portion; therefore I will wait for him."
~ Lamentations 3:22-24 (NIV)

As I am writing this morning, I am in beautiful and sunshine-filled Punta Cana, and I am struck by the amazing love Jesus has for me. Even though I have not done anything to warrant His love, He is deeply in love with me. Over the past few days I have met some incredibly beautiful, talented and wounded women who have shared their stories of pain and loss. But the one thing that resonates is the hope that there is something better, that there is more for their lives. And in the midst of trying to navigate my own journey, I am right there with them, wanting more.

Who among us does not desire to understand the fullness of God's love for us? If we could even grasp for a second the love He has for us, and the sacrifice of a painful death He made so that we could experience such depth of intimacy ~ then we would understand the breadth of that fullness. Our identity is found in Jesus. But what does that mean?

In John 4, there is the story of the woman at the well. She was a woman who had had many husbands, and was not even living with her current husband. Enter Jesus. I wonder how she felt? Probably very lonely, rejected and shamed. And here comes this man, Jesus, who walks into her life and tells her that she can have a more abundant life. But what about her past? What about the life that defined her existence? What about all that? Does that automatically get thrown away? Jesus knows her, loves her, and tells her that she can have life in Him. A new identity. If we were to base all of our identity on ourselves, our past, our successes, our failures, we would be a complete mess. *But, Jesus!*

Who is this man who would love us and give us an identity in Him? Imagine yourself as the woman at the well; you are having a conversation with Jesus, and He is telling you how much He loves you. How do you feel? What is He saying to you? Write down your thoughts.

Sometimes it is difficult to imagine just how much we are loved, and that the Creator of the universe thinks so highly of us. Our identity is found in Him, because of His love for us. Even when we fail and fall, He is still for us. The following passages of scripture are for your time of prayer and meditation. Start by asking God to show you the truth of these scriptures over your own life. Place yourself in the passage, and ask God to reveal truth to you. Don't hesitate to say the scriptures aloud, or to rewrite them, maybe you feel compelled to write your own thoughts, or draw a picture.

Keep me as the apple of your eye; hide me in the shadow of your wings.
~ Psalm 17:8 (NIV)

Lord my God, I called to you for help, and you healed me. You, Lord, brought me up from the realm of the dead; you spared me from going down to the pit. - Psalm 30:2-3 (NIV)

O Lord, you have examined my heart and know everything about me. You know when I sit down or stand up. You know my thoughts even when I'm far away. ~ Psalm 139:1-2 (NLT)

For the Lord your God is living among you. He is a mighty Saviour. He will take delight in you with gladness. With his love, he will calm all your fears. He will rejoice over you with joyful songs.
~ Zephaniah 3:17 (NLT)

I praise you because I am fearfully and wonderfully made; your works are wonderful, I know that full well. ~Psalm 139:14 (NIV)

Surely your goodness and unfailing love will pursue me all the days of my life, and I will live in the house of the Lord forever.
~ Psalm 23:6 (NLT)

Section Five

Time to Serve

> "Let us practise the fine art of making every work a priestly ministration. Let us believe that God is in all our simple deeds and learn to find Him there."
> ~ A.W. Tozer

At our church we talk a lot about becoming partners in the church and finding a way to serve in a ministry. It is a well-known fact within the church world that 20% of the people do 80% of the ministry. That fact is staggering to me, because in reality it should be the other way around. Part of being a part of the body of Christ (the local church) is relational and should involve your spiritual giftings and your passions. Often people come to church, partake in the service and then walk out the doors the moment the service ends. They are what we refer to as "consumers." As women of purpose, walking how God has designed us to be, we should be different from the average church attender. Now that you have discovered your giftings, have taken a look at some of your fears, and (I hope) are beginning to overcome, it's time to look at where God would have you partner.

If you're new to church life, and perhaps have never been involved in serving opportunities, it may seem a bit daunting. But let me assure you that getting involved in what God is doing in the life of your church is so rewarding. As long as you are walking in His desire for your life, you will feel fulfilled.

Unfortunately most people in churches have not really taken the time to see where they will fit best in ministry, and end up serving in an area that drains them of their time and energy. When this happens, burnout follows. I hope this course has equipped you with the tools to be able to recognize areas of ministry that suit your giftings. And with God's help, you will be able to navigate the ups and downs of serving.

Let me make one short disclaimer: there might be times in your life when God asks you to step out of your comfort zone and into something for which you do not feel qualified. Let me tell you, this has happened to me more than once. During those times, God may have a plan to grow your character and/or teach you a lesson or two. Or maybe there is a need in a certain area that must be filled by a mature believer. Whatever the case may be, allow God to speak to you in all circumstances.

There was a time when I began serving in a local church on the worship team. During that season, I was asked if I would play keyboard. Now, although I can play the piano, I am far more comfortable as a vocalist. In the two years I attended that church, I never once used my vocal giftings. Instead I had to work my way through the most difficult gospel keyboard parts known to mankind. I wrestled with God about it weekly, wanting to quit numerous times. But every time, the Holy Spirit convicted me to stick it out and keep on serving. And am I ever glad I did. The lessons learned during this time in my life have had an impact on my leadership and musical abilities, and have grown me as a believer. Never underestimate what God calls you to do!

What are some areas of ministry that you are serving in? Be specific as to whether they are within the context of the local church or the community.

During the past few weeks has God been stirring in you to partner in a particular ministry area? Describe what God is saying to you.

Outrageous Dreams

> **"You are never too old to set another**
> **goal or dream a new dream."**
> *~ C.S. Lewis*

Have you ever dreamt of something so outrageous that it did not seem even remotely possible that it would come to pass? When I was younger I dreamed BIG dreams, dreams that had me singing for thousands, dreams with my name on the cover of an album (or 10), and dreams where my name would be a household name. And even crazier than dreaming these outlandish dreams, was that I believed them! I hoped in them, put value all over them, and desired them to be true. Well, I am all grown up now, but I still hold on to some of those out-of-the-box dreams, ones that I know were birthed in my destiny. And even if I never see them come to pass, I always have the dream. Just today someone from my church asked me if my dreams were from another time in my life or could they still apply to my life today. (The answer is, "Some are, some aren't.")

More often than not I am astounded by the crazy life coincidences that just seem to happen. Although I am not really a believer in coincidences, I am a believer in God incidences. This journey of purpose for me has taken many twists and turns along the way, and I am not even close to where I thought I would be at this point in my life. Just when I think that I have something figured out, I am confronted with something else, and realize that I really haven't got that much figured out after all. Thank God that we don't have to rely on our own understanding, but only have to trust Him, the All-Knowing One, who also loves us beyond measure.

As I mentioned, I have had so many dreams for my future and hopes for my life. I would be lying to say that I have not been left disappointed that some of them have yet to come to pass, and quite frankly I hope for more than my present life seems to offer. There have been moments that I stop and wonder if there is more to life than what I am living, more that God has for me to do, more fulfillment and purpose.

Just this past week, I sat with a couple of friends at the local Tim Horton's after a Monday night young adult service at my church. I had really wanted to go home after an emotionally charged day, but felt compelled to meet my friends for late-night bagels with strawberry cream cheese. We soon got to talking about writing, and I learned that one of my friends is an accomplished writer. As I shared my desire to put down some God thoughts on paper for women, we got to talking about the writing process, publishing, and even how much writing I should be doing each day. Thoughts way too overwhelming for an amateur unpublished writer! And although I knew God had breathed these heart's desires for me to write, I felt totally ill-equipped to put them on paper.

Maybe you can relate. You totally know God is calling you to something out of the box, and really want to pursue it, but think, "How could He possibly want me to do it? I mean, how could He use little old me?"

Is there a dream that God gave you that you have long given up on? Does even the thought of a promise unanswered bring up wounds that need to be tended to? I have yet to meet someone who does not have a dream. Perhaps it is the dream of being a mother, yet each month you are left with an empty womb and devastated spirit. Could it be the dream of holding the keys to a new home? Or being hired for a position you feel unqualified for? Whatever the dream, big or small, God knows your heart and hears your cry. It is important to take the necessary steps of faith and obedience toward your dream.

I went through a season in my life where I began to doubt that God wanted to fulfill any of the dreams I had. Being unmarried with no potential prospects, feeling inadequate to fill ministry roles, and watching my life flash by me as though I were a spectator and not a participant, really made me feel doubtful and insecure about whether God was interested in me. I would love to tell you that I came through that season with flying colors, but that is simply not the case. If anything, it left me jaded and feeling pretty hopeless. But when God gives us a dream, it is not our responsibility to know the timing and understand why it has or has not come to pass.

One of the most outrageous dreams I've ever had was to be debt-free. There was a time in my life when that seemed like a very distant reality. I worried and fretted about how I would ever be able to live in financial freedom after having accumulated more than my share of school, credit card debt and immigration fees. I remember being in the prayer room of the Christian school I taught at and crying out to God. That morning my mentor, Jackie, and I had a conversation about the provision of God and she encouraged me to believe for the promises of God over my life. And within a year my debt was completely irradiated. Only God!! I often wonder why God chose to release me from that financial burden, and what comes to me over and over again is that He wanted me to see that His faithfulness toward me knows no bounds. I remind myself of this every time I begin to doubt that my dreams from Him are also His promises.

On the very first night of a Purpose Group, I asked the women to tell me about the biggest risk they had ever taken, but was not ready to answer the same question when they turned the question on me. I ended up fumbling for some sort of answer that would satisfy them. But what it left me with was a deep desire to push myself out of the boundaries of myself to take deeper risks, to feel more ~ to be open to the possibility of losing more to gain more.

On vacation to the Dominican Republic, I sat down with my friend Laura for dinner and together we made a list of 20 places and activities that I hope to accomplish in my lifetime. On my list was zip lining, and although for some people that does not seem risky at all, I am terribly afraid of heights. Even standing on my balcony has the tendency to freak me out. But the moment I was flying through the air at 50 km an hour through the jungle in the Dominican Republic, being afraid of heights was the last thing on my mind. Not only did I cross something off my list, but I conquered a fear and took a risk! And the next day I went parasailing!

Where & What List:

Let's start dreaming together. Make a list of 10 places you would like to go, along with 10 activities you would like to do there. This list is to get your mind activated and to let your creative side be unleashed. Now don't worry that you will have to accomplish these tomorrow, but I hope in your lifetime you will be able to cross off each and every one! In order to tap into your creative side, think about a place you've always wanted to go, or an activity you've always wanted to do. Here are a few examples from my own list: zip line in the Dominican Republic, take a cooking class in Italy, kiss the cod in Newfoundland, snorkel around the Great Barrier Reef, and sing in Madison Square Gardens.

Your turn! If you have more than 10 then by all means keep the list going and growing:

1. ....

2. ....

3. ....

4. ....

5. ....

6. ....

7. ....

8. ....

9. ....

10. ....

Dreams in Perspective:

Now that you have tapped into your creative side, let's go a little further and dream some big dreams. To help you in the process of getting to the heart of your dreams, we will look at them in the context of different categories of your life. Begin to ask God to help you dream something big for each area of your life.

Work *career aspirations*	
Living Arrangements *physical environment*	
Personal Growth *education, training, projects & development*	
Money *finances, investments, retirement & savings*	

Community
friends, neighbours, serving

Family
current & future

Health & Recreation
hobbies, healthcare,
mind/body/ spirit

God
personal relationship

Look over your "Dreams in Perspective." Which dreams are connected? Are there recurring themes in your dreams?

_____

_____

_____

_____

_____

_____

_____

Within these themes, which common passions emerge?

_____

_____

_____

_____

_____

_____

_____

Designing Your Life Message

**And we know that God causes everything to work
together for the good of those who love God and are
called according to his purpose for them.**
~ Romans 8:28 (NLT)

In the scriptures, Jesus talks about His purpose on earth. These few verses are power-packed with purpose and destiny. When we look closely at His life we can see that He knew why He had come to earth.

> *I am the gate; whoever enters through me will be saved. They will come in and go out, and find pasture. The thief comes only to steal and kill and destroy; I have come that they may have life, and have it to the full. ~ John 10:9-10 (NIV)*

Jesus refers to Himself as "the gate." In Biblical times, the shepherd was the gate for the sheep as he would lead the sheep into safety at night and then sleep across the opening of the sheep fold to keep out anything that might prey on the herd. The shepherd also kept the sheep from wandering out of the sheep pen and away from the herd. Here, Jesus is referring to Himself as safety, security; one we can place our faith in. And all throughout scripture we see that Jesus knew His life message.

Imagine the possibilities of what we can accomplish by the grace of God, through relationship with Jesus Christ and the empowerment of the Holy Spirit. You have journeyed through some tough assignments, navigated through your fears, and are beginning to come to a place of understanding of the woman God has created you to be. Recognizing that life is a journey in purpose will help you to hold yourself accountable, put your failures in perspective and move forward in your destiny.

I hope that at this point, you are proud of what you have been able to accomplish, and to see the beauty of who God has created you to be.

Don't forget to thank God for the success of this moment. And on those days that you are feeling hesitant to move forward, ask Him to remind you of your purpose. This is a great place for us to stop and write our own personal life message. A few phrases that encapsulate your giftedness, passions and purpose. It may take several tries to find the correct wording, and along the way you may change it as you gain more perspective. In a two- or three-sentence paragraph, write out your life message.

Life Message:

_____

_____

_____

_____

_____

_____

_____

_____

Power of Encouragement

The Lord will fulfill his purpose for me; your steadfast love, O Lord, endures forever. Do not forsake the work of your hands.
~ Psalm 138:8 (ESV)

Well, you did it! I am so proud of you for finishing strong, looking fear in the face, and walking forward into your destiny. I feel as excited for you at this moment as I was on the day I finished my very first 10k race. Crossing that finish line was monumental in my life, something I thought I would never be able to do in my life. In college I had failed my running class, and battling my weight for years kept me bound up in insecurity about ever getting fit. But that cool, rainy day in September I raised my arms as I crossed the finish line and was soon greeted by my family and friends who were there running the race alongside of me. I look back at all the times I was encouraged by my running partner Michelle and how much that relationship helped me to continue on. It is amazing what we are able to accomplish together!

It is so important that we journey this life together. No one walks or runs alone! Over the years, I have been tremendously blessed with great women in my life who have been a source of encouragement to me, and have kept my feet grounded in times of joy and discouragement. In fact, as I mentioned earlier, my very first mentor came into my life when I was only nine years old. Since then I have had many Godly women pour into my life their wisdom and courage, and because of these relationships, I am much richer. Some have been mentors, others have coached me along the way, and some, during times of healing, have counselled me.

As you continue on your life path, I hope you will choose to stay connected with the women you have been on this journey with. What a great joy to be able to do life with other women and know that there are others who can encourage you along the way. The bond that has been established will be one that may carry you through difficult seasons ahead, or celebrate great victories.

Along with the relationships you have formed with the women in this group comes the responsibility for you to stay the course and continue what you have started by finding a Godly mentor, coach or counsellor who will guide you through the next season.

What could you do if you had someone to help you along the way?

_____

_____

_____

_____

_____

_____

_____

_____

_____

_____

If you're looking for a mentoring relationship, you should look for a woman who has been able to walk through seasons of life and has been faithful on her journey. Find a woman of Godly character that will speak truth into your life, give you good sound counsel, someone you can pray with, who will encourage you on the journey, but most importantly someone you can do life with.

When looking for a coach, you should look for a woman who will assist you with making goals for the future, a Godly woman of character that will ask the right questions and give you the space you need to grow and mature as you make decisions that will affect your future. The coaching relationship may have its times and seasons, so being able to access that relationship when needed is always valuable.

If you're looking for a counselling relationship, then be open and vulnerable with the process, praying continually and asking God for the inner healing needed to overcome and have the victory that God desires for your life.

What relationship is God prompting you to pursue during this next season?

Made in the USA
Lexington, KY
24 July 2019